LIVE LIKE FICTION

30 Days To Become the Author
of Your Own Life Story

BY FRANCESCO MARCONI

Ordering Information:

Quantity sales. Special discounts are available on
quantity purchases by corporations, associations, and others.
For details, contact the publisher at the address above.

Printed in the United States of America. First Edition.

ISBN 978-0-9861483-5-4

For more information, visit: www.francescomarconi.org

For Rachel

Author's Note

THIS IS NOT JUST ANOTHER READ ON HOW TO SUCCEED.

I should know. I spent years plowing through book after book on success. The problem was that most of what I read didn't really apply to a 20-something young professional. These books were written by people at the apex of their careers, light-years removed from their early days of climbing the proverbial corporate ladder, and a little out of touch with folks like myself who were still on a journey to make an impact at work and in the world.

So I decided to take a stab at writing my own "success" story—a story that is still being written. Instead of a polished retrospective from the mountaintop, so to speak, I've drafted my own personal playbook of tested, real-time observations along the way.

I hope this book will be relevant for passionate professionals of all stripes. It might be seen on the gift table of your graduation party. It may be found in the backpack of a friend who just moved to the big city for her dream job. It might be kept on the desk or nightstand of a new hire. But it's also a book that rewards second and third passes.

You can pick it up at professional crossroads, when considering asking for a raise, when dealing with a demanding boss, or when simply craving an inspirational boost. This book is a life guide and a launchpad. It's a growth plan to fulfil your potential!

WRITE YOUR STORY.

Growing up in Italy, I was fascinated by stories of people who had found greatness by venturing to New York City. I read about artists like Andy Warhol and writers like F. Scott Fitzgerald, inventors including Samuel Morse, and businessmen such as Cornelius Vanderbilt. I wanted similar success, to create something from seemingly nothing, and take control of my destiny in the process. Inspired by these tales of triumph, I determined that one day I would move to the Big Apple.

The idea of living in a vibrant metropolis had become my most important priority. So much so that when I was 16, I bought a giant black & white photo of the Manhattan skyline and hung it above my bed. That was my way of creating a visual goal that I could engage with every night before going to sleep.

When I finally moved to city of my dreams for an internship, I didn't find the instant achievement I had hoped for. Disappointment slowly took over. I had no idea where to start my journey, what I wanted to do or even where I would live. It was time to recalibrate my goals.

My coping strategy was to focus on fitting in my new environment. I observed how people shook hands, how they behaved, how they made small talk. And I took hundreds of notes. Literal notes. What started as a social survival mechanism had turned into a real interest. I was researching communications, psychology and strategy. I was looking for a pattern.

You might call what I found an "algorithm," a formula that people use to find success. This algorithm is replicable. It is personalizable. I call it ENGAGE—one, because that's how the acronym worked out, but also because the point of this "secret formula" is engaging with your own life story, your purpose, and the people around you. It's about spending more time on the things that matter to you so that you get what you want in life.

In life, we often get tied down by what we think isn't possible. But when we take control of the story we tell ourselves, there are no limits. What if the secret to fulfilling your dreams meant knowing how to write your own life script—the kind that makes you memorable?

I've spent the last five years studying how stories can inspire incredible achievements. Now I am sharing how you can apply those same principles to help you grow your career from scratch.

Blunt, insightful and practical, this is the playbook for the curious and inspired! It's a blueprint of tested strategies to write your own narrative and find your path. To live like fiction, you will need to craft an ENGAGING story.

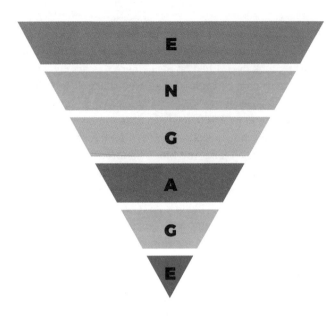

★ **DAY 1-5:**

EXPLORE YOUR MEANING

▼ **DAY 16-20:**

ANTICIPATE ROAD BLOCKS

▣ **DAY 6-10:**

NARROW YOUR GOALS

━ **DAY 21-25:**

GAIN PERSISTENCE

▲ **DAY 11-15:**

GENERATE A PLAN

•• **DAY 26-30:**

ELEVATE YOURSELF

SO WHAT EXACTLY IS ENGAGE?

ENGAGE is a six-step process for discovering what drives you and using it to succeed in your career. Many people's careers stall because they see strategic, high-level thinking, like knowing what their purpose is or what values drive them, as a "soft skill." They don't prioritize it. But that kind of thinking is exactly what enables entrepreneurs to launch successful startups, executives to get promoted and politicians to be elected. You can progress in your career without following this model, sure. But you'll eventually plateau.

IF YOU WANT TO BE NOT JUST GOOD, BUT THE BEST, ENGAGE IS FOR YOU. FOLLOW THESE 30 STEPS (ONE FOR EACH DAY OF THE MONTH), AND WATCH YOUR CAREER TAKE OFF!

WORKWEEK #1

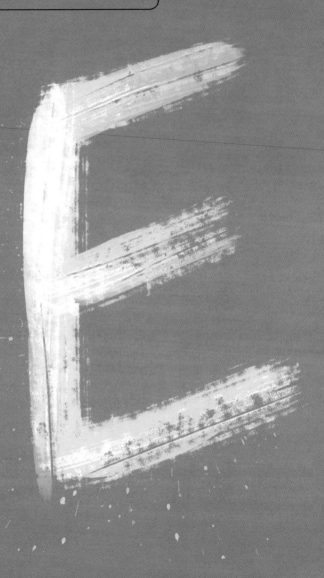

EXPLORE YOUR MEANING

Most of us start our journeys feeling lost. We ask ourselves, "What should I do with my life? Why am I working here? Am I in the right place?" The answers will appear only once you understand what gives **meaning** to your life.

DAY #1

FIND YOUR FOOTING

For young professionals, the "real world" can be paralyzing.
To find meaning, root yourself in your passions.
But how do you discover what drives you and find
your true professional voice?

"Whether you think you
can, or you think you
can't — you're right."

—**Henry Ford,**
Entrepreneur and industrialist

STUCK PUSHING PAPERS as a clerk at a law firm, recent college grad Lloyd Blankfein had no idea how he would move his career forward. But he knew one thing. Whatever task he set before himself, he would do it well. Eventually, Blankfein found a new stint as a salesman for a Wall Street trading company that was later acquired by Goldman Sachs. His passion for perfecting any task, no matter how small, would propel him to the top, earning him the title of CEO for the largest investment bank in the world.

Proof that Blankfein isn't just an anomaly comes from a global survey conducted by Deloitte. They asked participants what drives growth: purpose, or profit? An overwhelming 82 percent of respondents who worked at organizations with a strong sense of direction expressed confidence that their companies would grow.

In Blankfein's case, his drive to achieve excellence in everything—from selling concessions as a kid at Yankee Stadium to selling stocks on the global financial market—helped him turn purpose into profit.

The value of having a sense of purpose has actually been proven in scientific studies. A few years ago, Harvard psychologist Ellen Langer and a team of researchers put subjects in two flight simulators, one realistic, one broken. Participants in the first group were told to imagine themselves as pilots, and even given army fatigues to help them play the part. In the process, each group received an eye exam disguised as part of the simulation.

Langer's team found that subjects who "flew" in the realistic simulator showed a marked improvement in their vision compared to prior eyesight tests. What was going on? Langer concluded that pretending to be someone with good vision—like a pilot—could make our vision palpably better.

This means the power of our minds is, well, literally mind-bending. What if we choose to think of ourselves as creative? As confident? As good at sales? Exploring your meaning might mean deciding your meaning.

In my case, I chose to think of myself as someone who "decides with absolute certainty." So I wrote that phrase on a sticky note and keep copies on my desk at work and my fridge at home. Seeing that credo every day has enabled me to unconsciously make faster decisions.

THE TAKEAWAY: Think about what matters to you. What gives meaning to your life? We occasionally lose sight of our values—the things that define and drive us—and with them, our confidence in the future. If you aren't aligned with your values, it's easy to let limiting beliefs control you: I'm not smart enough, I don't have the resources, I'm not in a creative environment. But the reality is you are the X factor in this formula. If you change your mindset, you change yourself.

EXERCISE
BUILD YOUR CORE

Your values tell the story of how you see the world and surface
the things that are truly important to you. Circle the THREE most
important values from the list below.

Accomplishment	Friendship	Moral Fulfillment
Adventure	Health	Order
Appearance	Helping Others	Peace
Broadmindness	Honesty	Power
Community	Independence	Prestige
Competency	Influence	Purposefulness
Competition	Integrity	Recognition
Cooperation	Intellectual Stimulation	Security
Creativity		Self-Expression
Family	Intellectual Status	Travel
Fast Pace	Learning	Variety
Flexibility	Leisure	Wisdom
Freedom	Loyalty	

VALUES   What can I do in the next two weeks to get closer to my values?

EX.   ADVENTURE : Go on a day trip to the lake a with a friend

It's worth repeating this exercise at regular intervals, as one's
values do change throughout life. For example, you may start
a family, move to a new city or find something new that
inspires you!

DAY #2

KNOW WHY YOU DO IT

Your career is a medium through which you impact others.
How do you find meaning in the life story you are about to write?

"People will forget what you said,
people will forget what you did,
but people will never forget
how you made them feel."

—Maya Angelou,
Poet

EMMY AWARD-WINNING ACTOR Jon Hamm found success because of one lucky break. In 2006, director Matthew Weiner was looking for a "new face" who wouldn't command a high salary for his new show, "Mad Men," when he came across Hamm in an audition. Something sparked, and out of a field of more than 80 actors, the show's producers chose Hamm. Lucky, right? Well, maybe it wasn't just luck. Before becoming Don Draper, Hamm spent years waiting for his big break. He waited tables, taught drama classes and even worked as a set designer for porn films. He was growing older than most actors at the start of their careers, but Hamm says he had a voice inside of him urging him to keep going, that his time would come.

People like Hamm who see themselves as lucky—or maybe destined is a better word—are often the ones willing to take the greatest risks. And when the risks pay off, they pay off big. Take Elon Musk for example. Even as a college student, Musk knew how to describe his mission. The founder of online payments portal PayPal, electric car maker Tesla and space exploration company SpaceX gave up pursuing a Ph.D. to follow his entrepreneurial interest in areas that he says will "most affect the future of humanity in a positive way"—the Internet, sustainable energy and space exploration.

Okay, sure, we don't all look like Jon Hamm or have the vision of Elon Musk. But according to University of Pennsylvania psychology Professor Martin Seligman, feeling inspired at work is a much better predictor of job satisfaction than a big paycheck. Still, it takes more than having passion to succeed at work. Seligman argues that in addition to passion, taking on challenging tasks, enjoying supportive colleagues, using your skills and having a sense of purpose are key to your well-being in the workplace.

You might not have control over all those factors, but you can marry what matters to you with your work to find meaning and purpose in it. When people ask me what I do, I follow Musk's example. I don't say I work for a news company. I tell them I work for a company that "promotes democracy through news and information."

THE TAKEAWAY: When asked what your profession is, explain your job function and its emotional dimension. For example, maybe you work for an insurance company, and your job title is financial analyst. But your role, what you want others to know about what you do, is to ensure people sleep well at night because they know they are protected from loss.

EXERCISE
BUILD YOUR CREDO

Empathy and purpose are key drivers of today's workforce.
Ask yourself: What do I really do? What meaning do I find in it?
Who am I?

Draft a honest and positive response using the framework below,
then run your thinking by one or two friends.

I AM...

_____

_____

I FIND PURPOSE...

_____

_____

BONUS: AND ONE DAY I PLAN TO...

_____

_____

DAY #3

LOOK FOR
A HERO

Find someone in your life who encourages you to aim beyond
the ordinary. Whom can you look to for inspiration to aim
higher than you ever imagined?

"Heroes expand our sense
of possibility."

—**Scott La Barge,**
Philosophy professor

MARK ZUCKERBERG SAYS HIS HERO growing up was Bill Gates. He admired how Gates carried himself, how he built an empire. Zuckerberg ended up becoming like Gates, following in his footsteps by going to Harvard, dropping out of school, building a hugely successful company and devoting his life to philanthropy.

Five decades earlier and more than a thousand miles away, a young Morgan Freeman pinched pennies so that he could afford to go to the movies. In film stars like Gary Cooper, Sidney Poitier and Spencer Tracy, Freeman saw his own future career.

Of course, heroes don't have to be famous. Pablo Picasso said that his role model was his father, an arts teacher.

You need a hero, too. But simply choosing a role model, by itself, isn't enough to transform you into them. Psychology researchers have found that the real difference lies in how you understand leadership. According to the "Personality and Social Psychology Bulletin," if you believe leadership is something people are born with, comparing yourself to someone else who has succeeded in your field is unlikely to positively influence your own behavior—after all, how could you measure up? On the other hand, if you see leadership as a skill that can be practiced and improved, you're much more likely to benefit from having a role model.

You're more likely to treat skills you don't have as challenges rather than signs that you're destined for failure.

With that in mind, I've set my sights on becoming more like my heroes: my father for his creativity; my mother for her attention to detail; Arianna Huffington and Michael Bloomberg for building media empires from scratch; and chef Jamie Oliver for his passion for his profession.

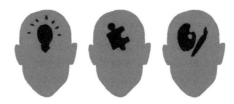

THE TAKEAWAY: Choose at least three people you look up to for their character, success or life philosophy. It doesn't matter if it's your mother, your college professor or your new boss, identifying a role model can be a source of inspiration. And remember, motivation isn't a fixed asset; you can always find more!

EXERCISE
IDENTIFY YOUR SOURCES OF INSPIRATION

Whom can you look to for help with aiming higher than you ever imagined?

Write down three adjectives you would like to be associated with, and match them with people you admire.

Draft an honest and positive response using the framework below, then run your thinking by one or two friends.

CREATIVE   **ANDY WARHOL**

_____   ▶   _____

_____   ▶   _____

_____   ▶   _____

_____   ▶   _____

DON'T BE A GROUCH

The power of positive thinking is immutable.
How do you train your mind to break free of
defeating thoughts?

"I am not what happened to me.
I am who I choose to become"

—**Carl Jung,**
Swiss psychiatrist

WHEN HE ARRIVED IN THE U.S., the 21-year-old immigrant barely spoke English. A few decades later, he had achieved worldwide fame as a movie star, an elite athlete and a successful businessman and politician. Arnold Schwarzenegger never doubted for a minute that he had a bright future ahead. The former Mr. Universe has been quoted often on his ability to project himself into his dreams of success: "When I was very young I visualized myself being and having what it was I wanted. Mentally I never had any doubts about it. The mind is really so incredible. Before I won my first Mr. Universe title, I walked around the tournament like I owned it."

For most of us, it's a lot easier to expect the worst than to imagine the best. But according to scientist and entrepreneur Trevor Blake, neuroscientists now know that exposure to negativity can actually impair the brain's ability to function. Even just 30 minutes listening to someone complain can deteriorate neurons in our hippocampus, the problem-solving part of the brain.

The good news is that a positive outlook can actually improve your health and your performance. In a 2010 Wayne State University study, researchers found that Major League Baseball players who smiled in their baseball card photos went on to live longer lives on average than those who did not—and the more intense the smile, the longer the player was likely to have lived.

Studies like these suggest that no matter how talented you are, if you're whiny, people are repelled by you. After all, you're hurting their brains! I used to work with a colleague who was thoughtful and knowledgeable, not to mention one of the most creative people I've ever met. But he had a habit of complaining about life, work, everything. People couldn't stand to be around him, and after a while, he ended up alienated from dozens of projects.

THE TAKEAWAY: Leave your private life (or career-related gripes) at the door of the office. If you need to scream, cry or complain, go for a walk. A positive attitude works like a magnet to attract promotions, raises and long-lasting relationships.

CONTROL NEGATIVITY

Having a positive attitude creates stronger aspirations. Train your mind to break free of defeating thoughts. Grab a sticky note and write down something that really frustrates you. Place the note in the box below.

Now, take the note off and tear it into pieces.
On the new note, write something positive that gives you inspiration each time you look at it.

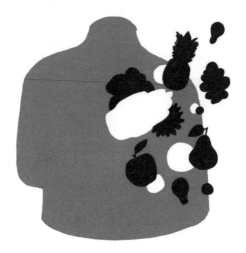

DAY #5

TELL
YOUR TALE

Storytelling is the most compelling form of communication, so
tell your story well and tell it to anyone who is willing to listen.
How can you use it to accelerate success?

"The universe is made of stories,
not of atoms."

—Muriel Rukeyser,
Poet

IN 2009, A MIDDLE SCHOOL ART TEACHER named Bre Pettis started MakerBots, a company whose product enabled people to print 3D objects that could be designed on any computer. As a new entrepreneur, he struggled to convince clients and investors that there was a market for his creation.

In response, he turned to an unusual strategy—storytelling. He shared with prospective company stakeholders the impact his invention could have. He talked about how health care professionals could save money by printing their own supplies with his tool. Then there was the student who used his teacher's printer to make himself a prosthetic hand.

Five years later, Pettis sold MakerBots for $604 million.

His theory that telling stories could make his ideas and business memorable proved to be correct. The numbers back him up: Jennifer Aaker, a marketing professor at Stanford Graduate School of Business, conducted a study finding that 63 percent of people recall stories a speaker shares, yet only 5 percent can remember a single statistic. In a different study, Aaker found stories to be up to 22 times more memorable than facts alone. They can captivate audiences, becoming tools of influence and persuading listeners to action.

Stories shape how others see you and could have implications for whether you are hired, go on dates or even raise money for your next business idea.

Scott Weiss, a prolific Silicon Valley venture capitalist, makes his investment decisions based on "how well the founder's life can explain what they're doing at their company." A person's path to greatness is often shaped by their own life experiences.

Stories have the ability to make an impact well beyond growing businesses—world leaders and iconic figures use them to speak to the wider public and explain complex issues. Martin Luther King Jr.'s "I Have a Dream" speech used storytelling to encourage people to imagine a more just and integrated society. John F. Kennedy rallied an entire nation around the idea of innovation and scientific progress by sharing his vision of sending a man to the moon.

Because I work for a news company, I often share my personal story about how my passion for the industry arose. It goes like this: My Italian father was on a train to Paris when he noticed a group of soldiers bothering a Portuguese woman as she was trying to read a newspaper.

He approached the soldiers, telling them to leave the woman alone. Then he wrote his phone number on the front page of the paper, saying, "If you are ever in Rome, give me a call and I'll show you around."

One year later, he received a call from the woman on the train, who was visiting Italy with a friend. She had kept the paper. That was the beginning of my parents' relationship—and why I can say that newspapers are in my DNA.

THE TAKEAWAY: Tell a story about yourself that evokes emotions. A good narrative translates an idea into an adventure, a romance, a thriller—and it sets you apart. Selectively shape it so that it's one people remember.

EXERCISE
CRAFT YOUR STORY

Imagine you sit down for a job interview, and the interviewer
says, "Tell me about yourself." Think about the things that drive
you and how your story can inspire others. Then follow this
framework to create your own personal narrative.

1. WHY are you telling the story?

2. HOW can you make the audience care?

3. WHAT will make other people share your story?

WEEKEND BREAK

Congratulations! You've made it through your first week on your journey. But what did you learn? Take some time to relax and reflect on what drives purpose in your life.

THIS WEEK'S TAKEAWAYS:

NARROW YOUR GOALS

Now that you know what your personal meaning is, it's time to **narrow down the goals** that will help you navigate through your career.

I INK,
THEREFORE
I AM

By writing your words you are infusing them with your existence,
far more so than with spoken words. What are you waiting for?

"Life isn't about finding yourself.
Life is about creating yourself."

—George Bernard Shaw,
Irish playwright

EVERYONE TELLS YOU THAT YOU need goals in order to succeed. What they don't tell you is just how hard it can be to come up with goals in the first place.

As a child, Thomas Edison had an incredibly imaginative mind, so much so that he was not able to focus in the classroom and eventually had to drop out to be homeschooled by his mother. Edison made it his life ambition to make her proud. But he tried many jobs, even selling candy and newspapers, before finding his true calling. What was it? Something that allowed him to draw on his dynamic imagination. The electric light bulb, the motion picture camera—over a thousand inventions with patents in his name have made Edison an icon for inspiration and entrepreneurship.

Edison chronicled his plans for new tools and technologies in more than 3,500 notebooks. He wrote out his ambitions and goals and achieved extraordinary results despite the lack of a formal education.

According to modern research, Edison's achievements may be due in no small part to his efforts to organize and document his ideas. Dominican University psychologist Gail Matthews found that you are, in fact, 42 percent more likely to fulfill your goals just by writing them down. In the same study, Matthews noted that if you send weekly updates to a friend, you are more than 70 percent more likely to reach your goals.

Here's a tip to get started: If you aren't sure what you want to do in life, think about the things that made you happy as a child and map them against potential careers. Write them down and be as specific as possible. While the goals you share publicly might be more re-alistic, don't be afraid to dream!

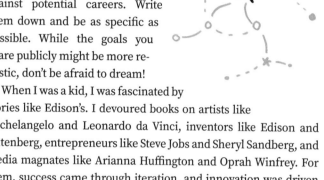

When I was a kid, I was fascinated by stories like Edison's. I devoured books on artists like Michelangelo and Leonardo da Vinci, inventors like Edison and Gutenberg, entrepreneurs like Steve Jobs and Sheryl Sandberg, and media magnates like Arianna Huffington and Oprah Winfrey. For them, success came through iteration, and innovation was driven by a desire for solutions, not wealth. Maybe most importantly, they weren't afraid to set ambitious goals and write them down.

Sure, it's difficult to know what you'll be doing five years from now, but it's important to at least be able to visualize your year ahead. I want to eventually become a senior executive in a me-dia company, and I've set goals for getting there. In the next three months, I want to complete a documentary series in virtual reality. At some point in the next year, I want to win an award or other rec-ognition for my work. And next year, I want to earn a promotion to lead the innovation department at my company. Ambitious, yes— but setting these goals for myself is the first step toward becoming an executive.

> **THE TAKEAWAY:** Still wondering why you should bother having clearly defined goals? After all, isn't knowing what drives you as a person enough? Not really. Setting goals keeps you from letting time slip past while you stay the same. It gives you something to hope for in the future while keeping you focused on the steps you have to take in the present.
> Big goals remind us of what matters.

EXERCISE
WRITE YOUR GOALS!

Seeing your objectives on paper helps you visualize your dreams. Write down the things you want to accomplish in each sticky note below:

THIS MONTH

THIS SEASON

THIS YEAR

EXPECT THE UNEXPECTED

Even the best plans fail. And that's okay. But how do you plan for the unplanned?

IN 2008, MICHAEL PHELPS was preparing to swim the 200-meter butterfly race at the Olympics in Beijing. He hit the water and immediately noticed that his goggles were leaking, slowly filling up until his vision was entirely obscured. But Phelps didn't stop or slow down. Phelps was prepared for this: before starting any competition, Phelps would close his eyes and imagine his next race, stroke by stroke, from start to finish. Now, as he swam blind through his last lap, Phelps knew instinctively how many strokes he had left. He approached the wall, gave a final push and reached out his hand the exact distance to touch the wall and win the race with a world-record setting time. Later, when a reporter asked Phelps what it was like to swim without being able to see, he replied, "It felt like I imagined it would."

Being prepared is not just an exercise for Olympic athletes, obviously. In my case, being prepared helped me get a raise. As I was returning to my desk from lunch one day, I received an unexpected summons from my boss to his office for a performance review. For a while I had been thinking about my contributions to the company and the value I brought to my team, imagining how I would frame my achievements in precisely this kind of situation. When I went into that office, I was able to ask for more money with clear and organized arguments.

Even the best-laid plans run into roadblocks, however. They may be people, circumstances, or our own limiting beliefs. They might even be tasks you have to complete to achieve a goal. Whatever shape these obstacles take, successful people learn to anticipate and navigate them by coming up with a Plan B. And having a backup plan can itself help boost your productivity, according to psychologist Tim Judge, who found that people who feel in control of their lives tend to achieve higher levels of performance in the workplace.

Sometimes our Plan B can turn out to be the best plan. Vera Wang just barely missed the cut for the 1968 U.S. Olympic figure skating team, a major setback in her athletic career. But Wang turned to her Plan B, plunging into the fashion world, and emerged an editor at Vogue. She went on to helm her now-iconic fashion design empire.

THE TAKEAWAY: Every day is the most important day of your life. Be prepared for the unexpected meeting that could make or break your career by mentally rehearsing your most effective sales pitch or presentation. And always have a question or comment ready for the most important person in your company; you never know when you two will meet in the elevator.

EXERCISE
LEARN FROM THE PAST

As we grow older, the unexpected becomes the expected.
Pick a moment from your past when life caught you off guard,
and write out how you responded to it.

What did you learn that can help you prepare for the
next unexpected event?

> **MOMENT**

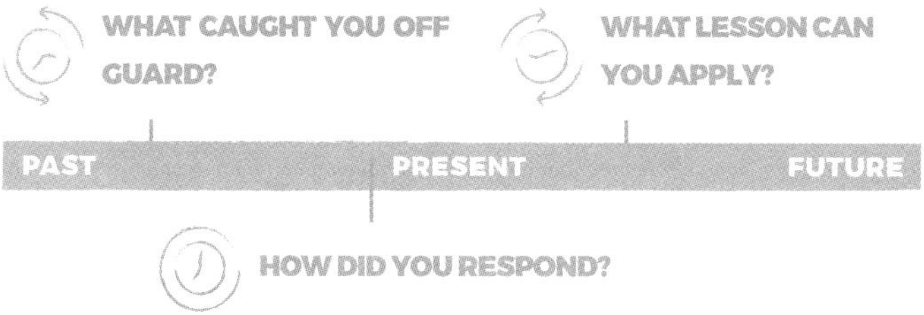

WHAT CAUGHT YOU OFF GUARD?   **WHAT LESSON CAN YOU APPLY?**

PAST   **PRESENT**   **FUTURE**

HOW DID YOU RESPOND?

○ **SURPRISE**

○ **RESPONSE**

○ **LESSON**

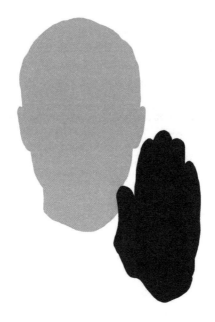

SAY NO TO SAY YES

Steve Jobs' creative and management process relied on a simple concept: Saying NO. How can you apply this sense of focus to your professional life?

"When you say yes to others, make sure
you are not saying no to yourself."

—Paulo Coelho,
Brazilian novelist

IN A STAPLES ADVANTAGE SURVEY of more than 2,500 employees, between 25 and 50 percent of respondents said they were feeling overwhelmed or burned out at work. Many of these same employees reported that if they just had more time, they wouldn't feel so worn down.

Unfortunately, even the ENGAGE algorithm can't conjure more hours in the day. But it can help you devote more time to the things that matter to you—by being selective.

Steve Jobs may be the most well-known proponent of this strategy. Jobs famous defined focus as not just saying "yes" to one thing, but also saying no to a "hundred other good ideas." According to Jobs, "You have to pick carefully. I'm actually as proud of the things we haven't done as the things I have done. Innovation is saying no to 1,000 things."

As a strategist, I operate like an internal consultant for the company. My associates ask for my help with projects ranging from marketing plans to financial forecasts and new investment opportunities in startups. At first, I took great pride in doing everything that was asked of me; after all, as a young professional, I wanted to show initiative. But over time the quality of my work suffered, and my colleagues became less interested in what I had to offer. What happened? I had become a commodity.

But I found the solution in economics, in the law of supply and demand. I became more selective about which projects I took on by simply explaining my priorities to others, and it wasn't long before the quality of my work improved—as did my reputation.

THE TAKEAWAY: If you can't bring value to a certain proposition or invitation, or to the project you are working on, shut it down with a powerful but polite "no thanks." Think it about this way: maybe you can create more hours in your day. Start by saying no and you'll find the extra time you've been looking for.

LEARN HOW TO SAY NO

Being selective in the tasks you take on brings a liberating sense of focus to your life. How would you say "no" in these tricky situations?

Someone asks you for help in a project:

_____

_____

_____

A friend asks you for a small loan of $100:

_____

_____

_____

You are invited to speak at an event:

_____

_____

_____

LEARN FROM GREATNESS

Discover more about yourself by studying the achievements of others. How might you learn from the footsteps of someone you admire?

"Through others we
become ourselves."

—Lev S. Vygotsky,
Scholar and psychologist

IF YOU CHOOSE TO TAKE A BEATEN PATH rather than blaze new trails, then you might as well follow in the footsteps of someone you admire. Jack Dorsey, the founder of Twitter and Square, Inc., is a good example. Dorsey emulates Steve Jobs in his style and conversation.

Like Apple's founder, Dorsey uses the expression "surprise and delight" to describe new products, he shares admiration for and inspiration from the Beatles, and he adheres to the philosophy of focusing on only one product and "putting other ideas on the shelf." When Dorsey talks about being fired from the company he founded, he borrows a phrase from Jobs: it was "like being punched in the stomach." Dorsey's mimicry has surely contributed to his reputation as a visionary like Jobs.

Mimicry also works at the micro-level, according to psychology professor Piotr Winkielman of the University of California, San Diego. With subconscious mimicry, you might find yourself laughing in response to another person's laughter, or crossing your arms when someone near you does the same. "Mimicry is a crucial part of social intelligence," Winkielman observes. But he also offers a warning: "It is not enough to simply know how to mimic. It's also important to know when and when not to."

My own approach is this. When I'm headed to a meeting with top executives at my company, I bring two notepads with me. With one, I take notes summarizing the discussion; on the other, I jot down interesting expressions I hear and could adopt myself. For example, I noticed leadership using phrases like "big win" and "having bandwidth," so I took them up myself. That way, when I present projects or share ideas, I speak the CEO's language.

THE TAKEAWAY: Look at successful people. Steal their interests, their passion and even their working style—but remember to always remain true to yourself. It's about trying on other's styles and seeing what feels right to you. If you are an aspiring journalist, be engaging like Megyn Kelly; if you are an entrepreneur, share your vision like Elon Musk. People will say you are the next *insert famous person in your field.* Of course, comparing yourself to the super-successful is aspirational and the path to get there may take some time. In the meantime, find a senior in your company you admire and find a way to work with him or her.

EMULATE SUCCESS

Following in the footsteps of someone you admire can
help lay the foundation for your own path.

Explore that person's back story, and write their life's path below.
How did they start? How did they launch their career? What did
they accomplish?

WHO IS IT?

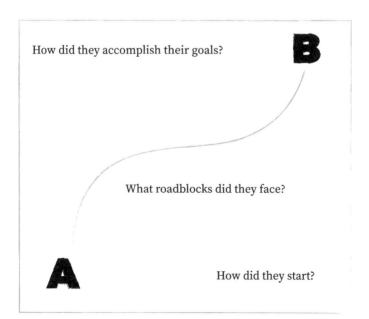

How did they accomplish their goals?

What roadblocks did they face?

How did they start?

KNOW YOUR STUFF

Achieving milestones comes from preparedness, which is correlated to confidence. How should you prepare?

"To be prepared is half the victory."

—**Miguel Cervantes,**
Spanish writer

A DESCENDANT OF WORKING CLASS IMMIGRANTS, Al Smith grew up in the early 1900s in the Lower East Side of New York City. Despite his humble beginnings, Smith was interested in politics, a profession usually reserved for the well-off. But Smith defied the odds and became a junior member of the New York State Assembly at age 31. At night, while politicians from aristocratic backgrounds attended parties and social events, Smith would read every single piece of legislation he could find. Eventually, senior leaders of the party noticed his preparedness and made Smith their trusted advisor. Smith went on to be elected governor of New York four times.

Like Smith, Zillow CEO Spencer Rascoff has a zeal to learn. Nothing is off limits for Rascoff—he wants to understand everything from social media to public relations, so he asks his management team to teach him. He even launched an internal speaker series at Zillow where high-profile executives of other companies can share their wisdom. It's no stretch to say that Rascoff's curiosity has helped Zillow become a billion dollar company.

You might not be a CEO of a billion-dollar company (yet), but no matter where you are in your career, one of the best things you can do is research.

In 2012, I was asked to give a TEDx talk about a small book I published on innovation. I had always been terrified of public speaking, and when I received the formal invitation, I gaped at the impressive lineup of speakers. Without a doubt I was the least qualified. I felt crushed under the weight of the names flanking mine on the program: one, a NASA astronaut, and the other, Brad Pitt's brother Doug, who does charity work in Africa. The pressure was on.

For a month I studied and memorized my talk, preparing contingency plans and pacing my presentation. On the big day, following the astronaut I walked up to the stage, looked at the audience ... and to my surprise, I felt entirely relaxed. I was ready for this. I was prepared.

THE TAKEAWAY: The fastest way to confidence is being prepared. Do your homework and read everything about your field or target audience. Knowledge workers such as lawyers, economists, managers, strategists and journalists are all in the business of selling air; your job is to make sure you convince people just how good your air is.

EXERCISE

GAMIFY LEARNING

Achieving your goals requires being prepared. Make learning enjoyable by setting rules and creating rewards.

EXAMPLE

TASK: Prepare a sales presentation for a client

RULE: I can only work on it between 9am and noon

REWARD: Go hiking this weekend!

TASK 1

TASK:

RULE:

REWARD:

TASK 2

TASK:

RULE:

REWARD:

TASK 3

TASK:

RULE:

REWARD:

WEEKEND BREAK

Your commitment to defining your personal goals will soon start to pay off! But where do you go from here? Think strategically about how to achieve what you want from your career before embarking on your first steps.

THIS WEEK'S TAKEAWAYS:

_____

_____

_____

_____

_____

_____

_____

_____

GENERATE A PLAN

Generating a plan of action can help chart your road to future success. How do you begin turning fiction into reality? This chapter provides the strategies to help you achieve your goals.

KNOW WHO TO IMPRESS

Focus on the people who can bring positive change to your life by showing them your true self. How do you make the most of your connections?

"Your focus determines your reality"

—George Lucas,
American filmmaker

AT THE AGE OF 19, Warren Buffett enrolled in Columbia Business School to learn from Benjamin Graham, the author of one of his favorite books on investing. Buffett focused on impressing Graham. His efforts paid off—Buffett was the only student to ever earn an A-plus in one of Graham's classes. A few years later, Graham invited Buffett to work at his investment firm in New York City.

Buffett identified the one person he needed to impress and focused his energies on that person. You should do the same. But you don't necessarily need to enroll in your boss's class to make an impression. According to research published in the journal "Social Cognition," you have about 34 milliseconds when meeting someone before they decide whether or not you're "trustworthy." And in those 34 milliseconds, it's all about your face: psychology researcher Peter Mende-Siedlecki found that smiling faces are more likely than angry-looking faces to be judged trustworthy.

So once you've figured out who you're trying to impress, don't forget to approach them with a smile and an encyclopedic knowledge of, well, them. Buffett had Graham; I had Miklos Sarvary, my professional idol and leader of the one of the top media research programs in the nation at Columbia Business School.

I decided to buy Sarvary's book and studied it as if I were preparing for the GMAT. Once I became an expert in Sarvary's work, I sent him an email, we met, and he invited me to become a scholar in his department. Later that year we launched the NYC Media Seminars, a conference series attracting the world's leading academics in media.

THE TAKEAWAY: For most people, things like meetings and emails eat up 90 percent of a typical work week, according to a recent poll commissioned by Adobe Systems. Don't waste time trying to impress everyone in the small amount of time you have left. Devote your day instead to impressing the person who can actually give you a promotion, write you a letter of recommendation or give you a raise. And always remember: you must ask to receive.

CENTER YOUR EFFORTS ON PEOPLE WHO MATTER

It's impossible to attend every meeting, answer every email and be able to complete all of your tasks in a workweek. Start making the most of your time by answering the following questions.

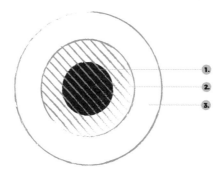

1. Write down one important goal you want to accomplish.

_____

_____

2. Who is the one person who can help you accomplish it?

_____

_____

3. How can you reach out to that person?

_____

_____

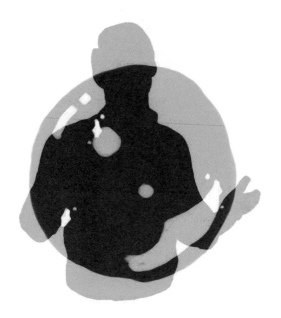

DAY #12

HUNT FOR CONNECTIONS

Managers hire and promote employees with "perceived similarities."
What specific traits do you see in your boss that you should emulate?

"Our Similarities bring us to
a common ground; Our Differences
allow us to be fascinated by
each other."

—Tony Robbins,
Businessman and author

AT ZAPPOS, THE ONLINE SHOE RETAIL STORE, CEO Tony Hsieh gives two different types of interviews to potential employees: one to test their job-related skills, the other to find out if they're a good fit for company culture. Hsieh's approach is really just a version of what most managers do without realizing it.

In fact, employers tend to hire people they'd like to hang out with, according to research conducted in 2012 by Northwestern University professor Lauren Rivera. More than 50 percent of employers listed "cultural fit," or perceived similarity to a firm's existing employees, as "the most important criterion" at the job interview stage.

This rule also applies to adapting to company culture once you have a job. I used to hate small talk. When I had to travel to a work conference in a car for two hours with a co-worker I didn't know, the first 40 minutes were awkward and uncomfortable. Finally I started asking questions until we both realized we shared a love for longboarding, of all things. We talked about it for hours, and the following weekend we went for a ride in Central Park. We eventually became good friends—all because I took the time to learn about him. I mined for interests until I found one we had in common.

This works for more than just alleviating awkward situations. Zoom out to get a big picture of your career. If you can identify the person who can help make your professional goals a reality, then start by researching that person. (Remember Day #11?) What traits, behaviors, and interests do you share? What habits can you learn and adopt from them? Successful people know how to adapt to the environment they aspire to be in.

And remember, standing between you and your goals is usually just one person—a boss, an HR manager, a professor, maybe even a potential investor. When that person is in your network, you need a plan to find what interests them.

> **THE TAKEAWAY:** Understand what people have in common with you, explore it, and use it to make introductions. When people look in the mirror, they see what they want to see; you should be the mirror that tells them what they want to hear. In other words, adapt your message for your audience.

EXERCISE

FIND A MATCH

Managers hire and promote employees with "perceived similarities." Which of your boss' specific traits should you emulate?

Draw a picture of your boss below, taking into account all of his or her traits, passions and characteristics. Does he like to fly fish? Include a fishing rod. Does she read four newspapers each morning? Include them. Now, do the same for yourself. Once you're finished, spot the differences between the two drawings.

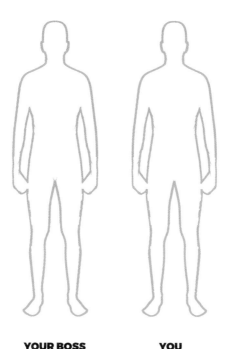

YOUR BOSS   **YOU**

BUILD YOUR CASE

Studying eloquent public speakers, journalists and business leaders points us to a perfect formula for building successful arguments. How can you effectively present your point to move ahead?

"The ability to simplify means to eliminate the unnecessary so that the necessary may speak."

—Hans Hofmann,
German-American painter

MOST STUDIES AGREE THAT THE AVERAGE PERSON remembers between 25 and 50 percent of what he or she hears. That means that when you talk to your boss, your colleagues or customers, they are likely to retain less than half of the conversation.

So how do you make sure you get your point across? Entrepreneur and former McKinsey consultant Ameer Ranadive believes the rule of three is what persuades his clients to take action. Ranadive smartly explains why this approach works: "1. Your argument gets their attention and is memorable. 2. You are forced to choose the three most important reasons. 3. You sound more structured, confident and decisive when you speak."

The three-point argument goes way back—like 2,000 years back. Ancient Greek philosopher Aristotle believed there were three essential elements to communicating successfully. Ethos, the first, has to do with the speaker's credibility or character. Pathos means appealing to your audience's emotions. Lastly, logos involves persuasion by means of reason, or logic.

These three Greek words have withstood the test of time in communication studies. Who knows, maybe the fact that there are three of them has something to do with how they've stuck.

In my own experience, the "rule of three" has helped me sound like I have an interesting opinion on everything, even on topics about which I know very little. When friends or co-workers ask, "What do you think about X?," I always answer, "Well, I can tell you three things about it..." And since my ideas are well-structured, they sound smart. (Now that my secret is out, use it to your advantage.)

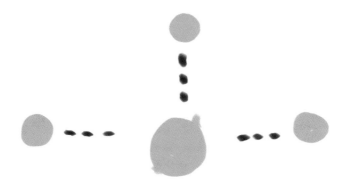

THE TAKEAWAY: Any answer, argument or presentation should be built around three main points. Do this and you sound informed but still keep things brief. And don't underestimate the little things—for example, when sending a report in attachment, summarize the most important information first.

USE THE RULE OF THREE

You can speak less and still say more. Imagine how would you effectively present the following:

Let's say you are tasked with implementing a new work policy at your office. From now on, everyone has to wear a feathered hat to work on Mondays. Use three arguments to explain why people should follow this seemingly strange rule.

ARGUMENTS

1. _____

_____

_____

2. _____

_____

_____

3. _____

_____

_____

MINE THE NUGGET

The world's biggest online publishers always look for the unexpected side of the story to attract and engage audiences. What specific steps can you take to build a following of loyal colleagues?

"Great stories happen to those
who can tell them."

— **Ira Glass,**
Radio producer

SINCE IT LAUNCHED IN SEPTEMBER 2012, digital news website
Quartz has achieved immense growth, reaching millions of engaged readers. How? By extracting the "golden nugget," the most
unusual or unexpected side of the story. For a story on pollution
and mislabeling in the tuna industry, for example, the Quartz
headline reads, "59 percent of America's 'tuna' isn't actually tuna."
Serving up the real meat of the story, so to speak.

To learn how to mine the "golden nugget" from a stream of
ideas, follow the advice of marketing Professor Jonah Berger. In
his book "Contagious: Why Things Catch On," Berger explains
there are six factors that lead to viral potential. An idea needs
to stand on its own, allow people to connect with everyday mo-
ments, inspire wonder and emotion, be publicly visible and replicable, provide practical value and create opportunities for a
shareable story.

When I first started working for a news company, I learned
this firsthand. The reports I sent to my supervisor, a former
business journalist, kept coming back to me with the question,
"What's the story?" The story—otherwise known as that gold-
en nugget—was always buried at the end of my write-up. This
is why my work wasn't getting noticed, my supervisor told me.
People were not interested in making the commitment to read
what I wrote unless I engaged them right off the bat. Once I began
mining the nugget, I finally received the recognition I had been
waiting for.

> **THE TAKEAWAY:** Always look for the most interesting angle. When you send links to colleagues, summarize the report with the most surprising or fascinating tidbit—the golden nugget—at the top. You save your coworkers' time and glean a conversation starter in turn.

EXERCISE

FIND THE NUGGET

Your personal stories can gain power if you follow the model used by the world's biggest online publishers. Build a loyal audience of your own by sharing ideas that resonate. Use the following questions as a framework to create viral content.

1. What is your idea?

_____

2. What strong emotion is associated with your idea?

_____

3. Can you add humor to your idea?

_____

4. What's something unexpected about your idea?

_____

5. Who can help you promote your idea?

_____

DAY #15

FORGET FOMO

Thinking you can do everything will lead you to the fear of missing out. How do you manage this infinite set of possibilities and keep focused on what really matters?

"You are the average of the five
people you spend the most
time with."

— **Jim Rohn,**
Entrepreneur and author

A STUDY LED BY ANDREW PRZYBYLSKI of Oxford University concluded that the Fear of Missing Out (FOMO for short) is higher in people whose essential psychological needs, including feeling loved and accepted, are not being met. And, according to Przybylski, "the workplace is a key area where FOMO is in play." But the inverse also holds true: the more passionate you are about what you do, the less FOMO you will feel, making you better equipped to manage your priorities.

According to Caterina Fake, the founder of Flickr and a prolific tech investor, FOMO isn't a new problem, but it is certainly intensified by social media. FOMO hits me hardest when I'm on Instagram or Facebook and see what my friends are up to—parties, travel, fine dining, and funny cats to boot—and want to join in. Out of FOMO I once accepted invitations to three different birthday parties all taking place within a two-hour time frame. I made an appearance at the first two parties but didn't really have time to enjoy myself and the company of my friends. On my rushed trip to the third party, I took the subway, only to get stuck underground for an hour with dozens of other people rushing to their own shindigs, during a hot and humid New York summer. It was horrible. I missed the last party and to this day I relate FOMO with feeling like a canned sardine.

THE TAKEAWAY: Don't let FOMO leave you chasing every opportunity that comes your way. Instead, choose quality over quantity and be selective about the events you attend, the information you read, the people you meet and the places you go. As "How I Met Your Mother" TV character Ted Mosby reminds us, nothing good happens after 2 a.m. anyway.

EXERCISE

UNPLUG!

Managing how you spend your time will keep you from FOMO. One way to stay focused is by going on a "digital diet." Choose and commit to one of the strategies below for the upcoming week:

○ Do not check your phone immediately after you wake up.

○ Do not check your phone before going to bed.

○ Read an amazing book instead of watching a TV show.

○ Have a meaningful conversation the next time you call your family.

○ Go for a run without listening to music.

○ Add your own strategy:

_____

WEEKEND BREAK

You learned that having a roadmap can help you chart a path for a memorable life story. Are you ready to start implementing your plan? Make sure you're prepared by reminding yourself of the way forward.

THIS WEEK'S TAKEAWAYS:

ANTICIPATE ROADBLOCKS

You've identified where you want to go and how to get there. You're ready to start. Now use these tips to **anticipate roadblocks** and to learn how to navigate unexpected situations from day one.

DAY #16

EAT THE BIG FROG FIRST

Don't miss out on something just because it is challenging. What's the best way to tackle complex projects?

"If it's important to you, you will find a way. If not you will find an excuse."

— Ryan Blair,
Entrepreneur and author

IN HIS LAST LESSON TO HIS UNDERGRADUATE students, "The Last Lecture: Really Achieving Your Childhood Dreams," Carnegie Mellon professor Randy Pausch shared his perspective on life while living as a terminally ill cancer patient. In one of his lectures, Pausch tells students, "If you have to eat a frog, don't spend a lot of time looking at it first. And if you have to eat three of them, don't start with the small one!" In other words, the professor was saying, do the most difficult thing first.

In the business world, this might also mean approaching the most difficult person first. I used to work with a colleague who always shut down my proposals no matter how good or bad—they were either "too expensive," "too incomplete" or "not necessary." My natural tendency was to avoid my colleague, but ultimately everything ended up on her desk. So I changed my approach and went directly to her, presenting my next idea in a way that made sense for her department. It was the first time she approved one of my proposed projects.

But you don't always have to swallow the frog whole, so to speak. Psychology researchers suggest that breaking a big, difficult project down into bite-sized, manageable sub-tasks with accompanying timelines is the key to avoiding procrastination.

Or you can take the more extreme path. French literary great Victor Hugo produced his epic (read: lengthy) masterpieces "Les Misérables" and "The Hunchback of Notre Dame" using one fail proof trick: he stripped naked in his study, then asked his servant to take his clothes and not return with them until the scheduled end of his writing session. (And this was before central heating!)

THE TAKEAWAY: If you are trying to sell an idea or project internally, go first to the colleague who is most likely to stand in your way. Show that person how your idea addresses a problem and explain the shared benefits it will bring to you both. Saying "You're the first person I came to about this" means Negative Nathan is more likely to put his guard down and endorse your work. The same goes for working alone: Do the most difficult part of an assignment first.

ACCOMPLISH YOUR MOST DIFFICULT TASK FIRST

Everyone has a to-do list they'd rather not look at. But checking off your toughest tasks will lift a weight from your shoulders and may even lead to a more fulfilling personal and professional life.

What's on your to-do list? Write it here and set a deadline to complete the first item.

	TO-DO	DEADLINE
○		
○		
○		
○		
○		
○		
○		

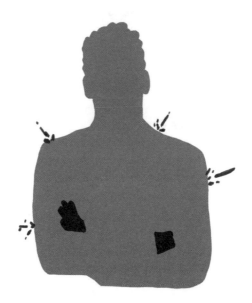

DAY #17

GROW A BACKBONE

People who tend to be more agreeable earn less than those who don't. How can you take advantage of your situation from day one?

"Weakness of attitude becomes
weakness of character"

— **Albert Einstein,**
Theoretical physicist

AN ACADEMIC PAPER PUBLISHED in the "Journal of Personality and Social Psychology" suggests that to some degree, nice guys—and gals—do finish last. The researchers examined earnings data to determine that men who rank high in "agreeableness"—how much you value getting along with others and how disposed you are to be critical of others—make up to $10,000 less per year than men who are less agreeable.

Growing a backbone isn't just about earning more money. It's also about your influence on the world around you. At what point will you stand up for yourself and for what matters to you? We often remember Nelson Mandela as South Africa's first black president, winner of the Nobel Peace Prize and an icon of freedom. But before all that, Mandela spent 27 years in prison for his anti-apartheid activism and political agitation against the state. Mandela went to prison for his ideals—and ultimately his imprisonment energized the anti-apartheid movement in South Africa.

You probably aren't facing a stint in prison for standing up for yourself at work or elsewhere. So what's holding you back? Start with the small things; in my case, I try to be courteous to everyone I meet and won't stand for it when someone isn't civil in return.

For example, several years ago I frequented a dry cleaning business with a clerk who was extremely rude to me and took ages to return my shirts. This encounter always left me upset. Finally it occurred to me to stand up for myself, so I walked in one morning and said, "Before you have the chance to be rude, let me remind you what I am paying you for: good, fast service!" After that, my shirts were ready on time and the clerk was always polite. Sure, I didn't enjoy being blunt, but growing a backbone actually improved my interactions with the clerk and the rest of my day.

THE TAKEAWAY: Show loyalty to others, but don't forget to be loyal to yourself. Involve yourself in your employer's interests, but not at the expense of your own. Speak up. If you are being taken advantage of, or you are undervalued, it's time to say something. And if someone is rude to you, tell him or her you won't tolerate it. Your confidence is the greatest deterrent for disrespect.

STAND YOUR GROUND

Let history again be your classroom. Think of a time when you felt insecure and/or someone at work treated you harshly.

What will you do differently the next time something similar happens? Practice with a friend the following actions during a mock disagreement.

Agree to disagree.

Explain why you deserve a promotion.

Speak up if you believe you are in the right.

DAY #18

GREASE IT WITH GRATITUDE

Helping others is a two-way street. When is the right time for you to start asking for what you want?

"The deepest craving of human nature is the need to be appreciated."

— **William James,**
Philosopher

ONE OF THE MOST PUBLIC DISPLAYS of gratitude each year, Oscar acceptance speeches are also one of the most closely-watched parts of the ceremony. Award winners always thank many people, ranging from film directors and event managers to their kid's kindergarten teacher. In fact, the list of "thank yous" has gotten so long in some speeches that the producers of the Academy Awards decided to change the format so that nominees can thank as many people as they want, using a scrolling list across the bottom of the broadcast.

Why is it so important to these actors that they thank all these people? Well, it's possible that all those thanks eventually translate into more Hollywood opportunities. Francesca Gino of Harvard Business School and Adam Grant of the University of Pennsylvania conducted a "gratitude experiment" to determine the effect of the phrase "thank you" in a reply email. They found that 55 percent of recipients to emails containing "thank you" felt an increased sense of self-worth, compared to 25 percent of people who did not receive notes that thanked them. The professors also found that 66 percent of people in the "gratitude group" were willing to extend help again when asked, versus 32 percent of the people who were not thanked.

I thought I'd conduct my own experiment on gratitude in one of my go-to lunch spots, a small take-out Indian restaurant on 9th Avenue near my office. At this place the servers assemble your meal in front of you, and if you're lucky, you get free pita bread with your order. To conduct my "experiment," I visited the restaurant for lunch every day for a week, making sure to say "thanks" after giving my order. I received a free pita bread every time I used the magic words. Coincidence? Maybe, but it certainly didn't hurt to say thanks.

> **THE TAKEAWAY:** Always end a conversation or exchange with a genuine "thank you." It's a simple but powerful way to make people feel valued and more willing to help you in future encounters.

SAY THANK YOU

Giving thanks helps you be in the present by noticing what you have and stopping to acknowledge it. Develop a habit of gratitude by attaching it to a part of your personal routine. Create a daily moment when to express three things you're grateful for!

I WILL PRACTICE GRATITUDE...

1.   When I am waiting in line for a cup of coffee

2.   When I am commuting home from work

3.   When I am running on a treadmill at the gym

4.

5.

6.

7.

8.

9.

10.

DAY #19

GIVE OTHERS THE FLOOR

We spend most of our time in conversation talking about our-selves. How do you take the first step to becoming genuinely interested in what others have to say?

> "People that know they are
> important, think about others.
> People that think they are
> important, think about
> themselves."

— Hans F. Hansen,
Football player

THE SPOKEN LANGUAGE IS THE oldest form of conversation, dating back 100,000 years. Has that impacted how our brain is wired?

Humans get a biochemical buzz from talking about themselves, according to a recent study by Harvard psychologists Diana Tamir and Jason P. Mitchell. Following the study, Tamir and Mitchell concluded that we spend almost 40 percent of conversation in "self-disclosure."

You don't have to be a Harvard-trained scientist to know that people like to talk about themselves. Jacqueline Kennedy Onassis became a PR master during her husband's campaign for the presidency and after he was elected in large part by being a world-class listener. She was known for being empathetic, present, open-minded and inquisitive. And when she spoke, in turn, all of America and the press listened up.

According to Kevin Sharer, the former CEO of biotech giant Amgen, knowing how to listen is one of the most important management skills. The former executive believes in the importance of switching from "listening with the sole purpose of replying" to "listening with the goal of comprehending".

I once had a meeting with a senior executive who had asked for my help with a research report. The next day he told me I was the brightest talent he had met in years. I was astonished—I only spoke twice during our entire meeting, once to ask "How can I help?" when I sat down, and then "When do you need it by?" just before leaving his office.

THE TAKEAWAY: Let people talk about themselves—it's the easiest and best way to make a good impression. Ask simple questions, and then ask more questions. Trouble with small talk in the elevator? Use the magic question: What have you been working on? People are always excited to tell you about their projects.

BE THOUGHTFUL

Asking simple questions is a meaningful way to build trust and strong relationships with others.

Write questions you would use for each of the following circumstances.

You share an elevator ride with the CEO of your company:

You bump into a former colleague who recently left your company:

You meet the presenter of a conference you just attended:

GIVE BEFORE YOU ASK

People tend to return a favor if given help first. But whom do you help in the first place?

"No one has ever become
poor by giving."

— Anne Frank,
Diarist and writer

IN HIS BOOK "Influence: The Psychology of Persuasion," psychologist Robert Cialdini describes the concept of "reciprocity," in which people tend to return a favor. Cialdini cites a Hare Krishna tactic of offering unsuspecting travelers a flower, saying it is a gift. Once the tourist accepts the flower, the disciple requests a donation—and most of the time, the tourist hands it over.

Hare Krishna devotees are certainly not the first people to practice "reciprocity." In ancient Greece, direct reciprocity was the way citizens exchanged goods. When the recipient lacked anything to give in return, then they engaged in "deferred reciprocity," or the expectation that the recipient of a gift will return the favor later, when the giver is in need. This was especially common among travelers. We see this idea illustrated in Homer's epic poem the Odyssey, as Odysseus depends on the generosity of those he meets along his journey home.

In modern times, we call deferred reciprocity "paying it forward." A 2010 study by University of San Diego professor James Fowler discovered that beneficiaries of generosity are likely to be generous themselves in the future. In fact, giving one dollar to a stranger had ripple effects, leading the researchers to conclude that one small gesture may ultimately yield three times as much additional generosity.

Eventually, what goes around, comes around—even if it takes a detour or doesn't look like what you expected initially. A senior executive at my company, for example, always stopped by the office vending machine for a mid-afternoon bag of pretzels. One day I noticed that the machine had run out, so I dashed across the street to a nearby stand for pretzels so he could still enjoy his favorite snack. Later that day he approved one of my proposals. Coincidence?

THE TAKEAWAY: Build your social capital before asking for a favor. The simplest way to do this? Offer to do something that is easy for you but difficult for the other person, whether that is picking up a cake for the office party, developing a business plan, or creating a marketing campaign.

EXERCISE

BUILD A "GIVING" PORTFOLIO

People tend to return a favor if given help first.

Think of three skills you have, such as writing a cover letter, designing a logo or building a financial budget. Whom can you lend a helping hand?

SKILL

RECIPIENT

WEEKEND BREAK

This week, you learned how to manage unforeseen life circumstances. How'd it go? If you feel you can use some more practice, use this page to hone your new skills. Like anything else, the more you can apply something to your life, the more natural it will become to you.

THIS WEEK'S TAKEAWAYS:

GAIN PERSISTENCE

Motivating yourself to keep writing your story can be harder than starting a journey in the first place. How do you avoid getting burned out? These lessons will help you keep your eyes on the target so you never give up.

BE BOLD

In life and in business, all opportunities start at the end of your comfort zone. How can you keep pushing until you get what you want?

> "Passion and persistence
> will solve almost anything."

— Ben Franklin,
Author and Politician

ONE OF MY FAVORITE FILMS, "The Pursuit of Happyness," tells the story of Chris Gardner, a man who went from life on the streets to becoming a multi-millionaire. He got his start as a trainee at the financial firm Dean Witter Reynolds, where he would call 200 potential clients a day. By being tenacious, Gardner rose in the ranks of the company and went on to become a successful entrepreneur and author.

In a different industry, brothers Matt and Ross Duffer kept pushing for their script to get picked up by TV networks, seemingly to no avail. Their show about the crossover between a parallel universe and small-town life in 1980s Indiana kept getting rejected—15 to 20 times. Still, the Duffer brothers' persistence outweighed the rejections. Eventually, "Stranger Things" found a home on Netflix and went on to become one of the most popular new shows of 2016.

Being pushy doesn't come easily to me. But to get my job as a corporate strategist, I forced myself to send more than 10 follow-up emails after my interviews to keep myself at the front of the hiring manager's mind. Although I didn't enjoy being pushy, it paid off in the end: after I was hired, the recruiter told me that HR liked my perseverance.

So how do you build perseverance? Psychologists who study cognitive flexibility argue that the answer has to do with being open to the unexpected—even if that's just trying a new restaurant, meeting new people, or discovering a new hobby. When you feel like giving up, switch things up instead. Do something totally out of your wheelhouse—it doesn't even have to align with your goal. Are you struggling to get recognized at work? Learn to cook a new recipe, change the route you take on your commute, try a new sport, or simply spend your lunch break with someone you haven't met before.

THE TAKEAWAY: Remember that you are always selling yourself, even if that requires going the extra mile. For example, send a follow-up email after conversations or meetings with colleagues. This acknowledges the conversation and the impact it had on you.

EXERCISE

STEP OUT OF YOUR COMFORT ZONE

You grow the most when you step outside your comfort zone. Use the note below to write a word that you need to confront (e.g. networking). Say it out loud and then talk with a friend to come up with a strategy to help you tackle it.

KNOW WHEN (NOT) TO TALK

Productivity at work increases when there are no interruptions. How can you resist the urge to talk to others and become more tenacious?

"Honey, once you've made the sale, stop selling."

— Marshall Eriksen,
How I Met Your Mother

AT THE BEGINNING OF EVERY DAY, Vijaw Eswaran spends an hour in silent meditation. The Malaysian business magnate and Q1 Group chairman uses that hour of silence to focus on his long-term goals and reflect on progress and failures; he claims that his success stems in no small part from the practice of silence.

For Eswaran, and for every person working in an office, silence makes good sense. In a study on task-switching and interruptions, researchers for Microsoft Corporation recorded the activities of information workers. They found that participants were interrupted four times per hour on average. Not unexpected, right? But get this: 40 percent of the time the interrupted individuals did not resume the task they were working on before they were disturbed. In fact, critical long-term projects were even more difficult for the workers to return to.

This happened to me. At the beginning of my career I felt the need to interject myself into discussions to prove I had something to offer. When I joined a team working on a proposal due the following week, however, I quickly noticed a change in the behavior of my peers in response to my constant editorials, as the initially welcoming atmosphere devolved to a high-pressure environment.

At first I thought I wasn't contributing enough, so I jumped in even more frequently than before. We missed our deadline—and I later understood it was my fault.

THE TAKEAWAY: In Western culture, people have the tendency to fill up quiet space with unnecessary chatter. Resist that urge. Be patient, and when you have almost convinced someone your way is best, say little, or else you risk that person changing his or her mind. If a meeting is wrapping up on a positive note, save your questions for later. And if someone is working on a challenging task, don't interrupt him or her. Knowing when to shut up increases your productivity and your co-workers'.

EXERCISE
STOP TALKING

Practice active listening. Think of a person who makes your wheels start spinning furiously in anticipation of what you want to say in response. Is it your boss? The colleague sitting next to you? Rather than preparing your own rebuttal, make a point to listen. You'll be amazed at how much you'll learn about them.

Now list three people who you need to practice active listening with.

ACTIVE LISTENING LIST...

EX: My manager

SAVE YOUR STRENGTH

"Decision fatigue" notes the decline in cognitive ability after making a series of micro-decisions throughout the day. How can you stay alert throughout the day?

"Rituals are the formulas by
which harmony is restored."

— **Terry Tempest Williams,**
American author

IN 2012, PRESIDENT BARACK OBAMA revealed one secret to his success—he wore only gray or blue suits. According to the president, he didn't want to waste mental energy on deciding what to pull out of his closet each morning when he had much more important decisions to make later in the day.

Tech billionaire Mark Zuckerberg goes one step further, wearing the exact same style of gray T-shirts and hoodies each day. "I want to clear my life," he said, "to make it so that I have to make as few decisions as possible about anything except how to best serve the Facebook community."

According to a study by Columbia University researcher Sheena Iyengar, the average individual makes approximately 70 daily decisions, with roughly half related to work. Because we have to navigate so many choices in our lives, it's important to eliminate ones that can become part of a routine or a ritual. Doing so enables you to reduce the number of decisions you make and to increase the amount of focus you can provide to the ones that remain.

Saving your strength can be accomplished by choices beyond what to wear. Square and Twitter CEO Jack Dorsey and AOL CEO Tim Armstrong start every day the same way by working out.

Whole Foods founder John Mackey makes a breakfast smoothie each morning with fresh fruits and vegetables.

It's also important to act quickly rather than to over think decisions, according to a study by Saras D. Sarasvathy of the University of Virginia's Darden School of Business. Sarasvathy posits that one common behavior of successful entrepreneurs such as Zuckerberg is their tendency to act rather than to overanalyze.

Decision-making builds momentum and inspiration—the development director for the think tank Talent Smart, Nick Tasler, found that an unexpected decision to cut back on an old habit in favor of doing something new can itself be a catalyst for change. The CEO of Starbucks, Howard Schultz, temporarily removed breakfast sandwiches from his stores to refocus his employees on making great coffee.

I find that putting one small part of my life on autopilot has had enormous benefits for the rest of my workday. Every morning for the past three years, I have followed the same routine, including the way I get dressed, the bowl of fruit I eat and the route I take to work. Waking up and getting ready this way starts my day off efficiently and leaves me energized to make decisions when I arrive at the office. And once I'm there, I'm always greeted by the sticky note on my desk that reminds me to "decide with absolute certainty."

THE TAKEAWAY: Follow the lead of Obama and Zuckerberg and eliminate as many trivial decisions as you can from your life. With everything else, don't waste your time pondering—just decide!

PUT YOUR LIFE ON AUTO-PILOT

Save time and energy on trivial decisions. Pick one of the following routine tasks to streamline for next week.

LUNCH
Make a big batch of something healthy and tasty to take to work a few days this week.

CLOTHING
Lay out or mark the clothing you plan to wear to work this week.

AUTOMATE
Figure out one thing that can be automated in your life, such as setting an alarm for the coffee pot.

GET CREATIVE
Have fun with it! Altering small decisions here and there can be the catalyst for change elsewhere in your life.

DAY #24

MOONLIGHT

What you do for fun can boost performance and productivity at work. Can hobbies really accelerate your professional success?

"The cure for boredom is curiosity.
There is no cure for curiosity."

— **Dorothy Parker,**
Poet

MANY SUCCESSFUL PEOPLE USE their creativity to propel projects from point A to point B. But where do they get that spark of curiosity? According to Carol Kauffman, an assistant clinical professor at Harvard Medical School, it comes from what you do outside the office. Neurologists and psychologists agree that when you get lost in a hobby or project seemingly unrelated to work —like crafting, painting or running—the part of your brain dedicated to creative thinking fires up, helping you stay focused and energized. And the benefits of hobbies' brain-boosting powers go beyond that killer scrapbook you made. They can increase your problem-solving skills and inspire new ways of thinking, meaning that your hobbies can be your greatest professional assets.

According to research published in the "European Journal of Work and Organizational Psychology," though, many people don't recognize the importance of leisure time. They use their downtime to "escape" from work and turn to passive consumption like watching TV or hitting the bar rather than creative activities. In the long term, the researchers note, this type of behavior can contribute to apathy and depression. But creative side projects and hobbies can help stop this cycle—they make downtime more fulfilling. They give you a broader perspective on life.

In fact, San Francisco State University psychology professor Kevin Eschelman found that people engaged in creative activities perform 15 to 30 percent better at work thanks to a better "sense of relaxation and control."

Hobbies are so important that well-known figures across all industries use them to refocus their mind. Music star Taylor Swift finds time to needlepoint while on tour, while actress Meryl Streep is an expert knitter. David Rockefeller, a former chairman and CEO of Chase Manhattan Corporation, collects beetles. As a teenager, Facebook founder Mark Zuckerberg built computer games for fun from the designs of artist friends; he even claims that Facebook itself began as a "hobby." Former U.S. Secretary of State Condoleezza Rice is an avid golfer. Albert Einstein enjoyed sailing. Actress Susan Sarandon loves to play table tennis. Even former President George W. Bush is known for his dabbling into portrait painting.

While the list goes on, the best part is that you don't have to be rich and famous to enjoy a hobby. Mine is watercolor painting. I sit at my desk at home and study my pet fish, Sushi, for inspiration. Then I draw different shapes and colors, an abstract exercise, until I enter the "zone." This helps me relax and return to work more focused and creative.

Later I take my "masterpieces" to work, because as Eschelman noted, small changes to your workspace can also make the difference and energize your life. Entire companies even do this, including Zappos.com, which incorporates employee artwork in the office and organizes creative workshops to help workers relax and recharge during the day.

Hobbies can also make you more interesting; several of my colleagues at work are known for more than their job descriptions. I work with surfers, aspiring artists, barbeque masters, mountain hikers and bikers, rock band leaders and marathon runners. A software engineer brings his guitar to work on Fridays and serenades anyone walking by the cafeteria. A talented journalist and skilled baker shares her cakes with the rest of the office. That diversity is what makes our team so interesting—and serves as a reminder that what we do at work doesn't define who we are.

THE TAKEAWAY: A hobby can yield better work performance and stronger personal and professional relationships. It also makes for a great story, especially if you can find something memorable. If you don't have one yet, find one. It will help you become more productive in your day job and spice up office small talk.

EXERCISE
FIND A HOBBY

A hobby can boost your productivity. Coloring detailed illustrations is a simple activity that can help with stress relief and relaxation. Fill out the drawing below while brainstorming possible regular hobbies. Here are a few ideas to get you started: screenprinting, dance classes, windsurfing, book club, cycling, GIF-making, stamp collecting...

Write down other possible hobbies:

1. _____

2. _____

3. _____

FIND YOUR ZEN

Disconnecting from the buzz of the outside world has positive psychological effects and keeps you focused. Where can you go to unwind besides a Buddhist temple?

"A calm mind brings inner strength and self-confidence."

— **Dalai Lama,**
Buddhist monk

OPRAH DOES IT. Paul McCartney does too. As do philanthropist Ray Dalio, actor Hugh Jackman and Marc Benioff of Salesforce.com. Throughout history, some of our most powerful and prominent people have been, yes, meditators. As the founder of investment management firm Bridgewater Associates, Dalio believes taking time to disconnect and relax in meditation has made him more efficient—"like a ninja in a fight," he says. Benioff relied on meditation to manage stress while he was working at multinational tech company Oracle. And Oprah Winfrey has meditated daily after inviting meditation teachers to her studios to guide her and her staff in meditative practice twice a day. According to Oprah, meditating "changes the energy of everybody in your company."

Research supports the idea that meditation—or quiet time—leads to stress prevention. Just one example: Children who sit quietly for short periods of time experience a 40 percent reduction in stress and a 10 percent increase in test scores, according to the David Lynch Foundation.

Every morning I sit in a red chair in my room and close my eyes for 20 minutes. I use this time to regroup my thoughts and visualize the day ahead, and slowly I let go of any stress from the day before. Since I've started this simple routine, I feel much more calm, focused and creative.

THE TAKEAWAY: Take time to be with yourself and disconnect from the buzz of your phone, email and Twitter. Even if it's only for 15 minutes, start your day by sitting in a quiet room with your eyes closed. Use this time to recharge and think of what you need to accomplish during the workday. You will come out refreshed and ready to tackle what's ahead.

EXERCISE
MEDITATE

Disconnecting from the buzz of the outside world carries positive psychological effects and keeps you focused. Set a timer on your phone for 10 minutes; sit straight on a comfortable chair and close your eyes. Allow your thoughts to arise and watch them float by like clouds, or like birds flying in the sky. I wouldn't recommend this if it didn't work wonders for me.

What's your state of mind after meditating?

WEEKEND BREAK

You are now in possession of the strategies to keep yourself motivated and push forward. It's OK to enjoy a hard-earned day off—but, first, take a minute to reflect on lessons learned.

THIS WEEK'S TAKEAWAYS:

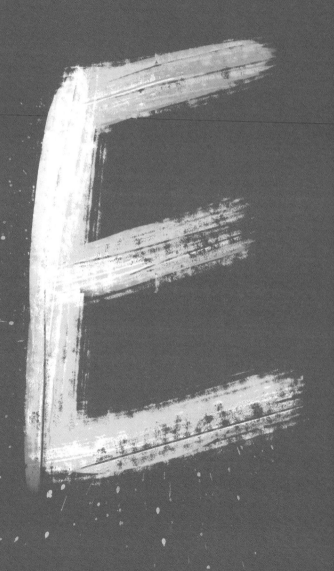

ELEVATE YOURSELF

The hard work you are putting into authoring your life story will elevate you to a place where you will be looked up to. How do you become a role model and help others with their own goals? Follow these tips to inspire your colleagues and build a long-lasting following.

DAY #26

IMPROVE YOUR CREDIT REPORT

Employee and peer recognition is the key driver of individual performance. How do you inspire others?

"Be an encourager.
The world has plenty of
critics already."

— Dave Willis,
Teacher and world traveler

WHAT ARE PEOPLE'S MOST BASIC NEEDS? According to Abraham Maslow's famous psychological theory, two of humans' most fundamental needs are the need to belong and the need to be appreciated. If you're a leader—and if you follow the ENGAGE formula, you'll soon find yourself in a leadership position—you have the opportunity to meet these needs in other people. This probably seems daunting, but becoming a leader who inspires people does not necessarily call for grand gestures. It means paying attention, saying thank you, and recognizing the work others have done.

A thoughtful compliment can go a long way towards inspiring others. It's no accident that Bill Clinton frequently acknowledges his high school band director as not only helping him grow as a saxophone player, but as a leader. Or that Ronald Reagan chose to write his touching open letter to the American people in 1994 after being diagnosed with Alzheimer's disease. Or that President Obama, after reading Yann Martel's book "Life of Pi," sent Martel a thank-you note praising his storytelling and powerful message.

Oil baron John D. Rockefeller also knew the power of saying thank you. Rockefeller once discovered his employees smoking where it was not allowed. But Rockefeller didn't bark at the men.

Instead, he joined them and accepted a cigarette. Then he told his workers that their work was appreciated and asked good-naturedly if next time they would smoke elsewhere.

Rockefeller knew that people like to be acknowledged for their work even when they make mistakes. Today's top executives know this too: According to the Aberdeen Group, a majority of best-in-class organizations rank employee recognition as extremely valuable in driving individual performance. This matters outside the office too. A study by Stanford University psychologist Sonja Lyubomirsky found that students who performed five random acts of kindness, such as praising others, each day reported higher levels of happiness than those who did not.

I found this tenet to be true when I led a small team of designers and programmers in the Hearst Media Design Competition. It was an all-star cast, with one wild card, who struggled to keep up with the other team members. So I became his cheerleader. I praised his progress every single day; I texted and called him to say how well he was doing. Within two weeks, his improvement was unbelievable. He was working better, faster and more creatively. He even proposed a solution for a complex problem we encountered at the beginning of the project. Our team went on to win the competition and present our work to the chief technology officer at Hearst.

THE TAKEAWAY: Give peers their due credit, and then some more. Make connections between their input and your own. Using six simple words—"This goes back to your point"—you acknowledge that you were listening to and value the other person's opinion.

BE AN ENCOURAGER

A thoughtful compliment can go a long way toward inspiring others and increasing your leadership skills. Add your own comments of praise to those listed below.

- You have the best ideas.

- You always know what to do.

- Your style is impeccable.

- Your thoughts are strategic.

- Your ideas are inspiring.

- Your style is flawless.

- Your intuition is correct.

- _____

- _____

- _____

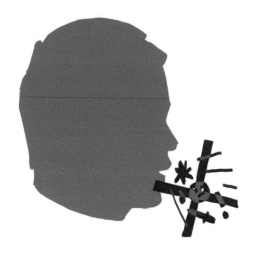

TRASH THE TRASH TALK

Individuals take on the personality traits they use to describe others. How do you build strength of character by avoiding disparaging others?

> "Promote what you love instead
> of bashing what you hate."

> — **Ron Oliver,**
> Writer

WHAT IF THE REASON COMPANIES FAIL is because workers are worried? Worried about the mistakes they made in that policy directive, the time they misspoke in that meeting, the way so-and-so colleague seems to be a lot chummier with the boss than they are. For the research software firm Qualtrics, workers' tendency to dwell on their mistakes or spread rumors about others posed a major threat to the company's future. So Qualtrics implemented a bold plan: They made all employees' performance data public to anyone in the company. No more concerns that the wrong people are getting all the big promotions, or that your hard work will be overlooked. No more watercooler gossip—it was all right there for everyone to see.

Some people cope with their worries by projecting their angst outward onto other people. A close friend of mine was very popular in college, wowing faculty and students with his academic and athletic performance. But he also excelled at criticizing people—to the point that it came back to bite him. Before graduation, my friend applied to his dream job at a top marketing firm. He was the ideal candidate. He aced the interview.

But the company turned him down. Shocked, he later discovered that other recent hires knew about his reputation as a sidewalk superintendent and  advised the hiring manager to choose a different candidate.

Badmouthing your colleagues may have other unintended consequences. A team of psychologists from the United States and New Zealand coined the term "spontaneous trait transference" for the way individuals take on the personality traits that they use to describe others. According to the psychology of spontaneous trait transference, if you tell your friend that someone you both know is selfish and self-centered, she will unconsciously associate you with those two negative characteristics. The worst part is that such associations persist over time!

> **THE TAKEAWAY:** My friend learned the hard way that criticizing others is a sign of a lack of self-awareness. Show respect to your coworkers and be straightforward with them when you notice a problem.

CHANGE THE NARRATIVE

Making negative comments about someone else devalues your reputation. Take a sticky note and write an example of trash talk you've used in the past, then really listen to yourself as you say it out loud.

NOW, THROW THE POST AWAY AND AVOID SAYING IT AGAIN!

DAY #28

BE A
BOW TIE

Unusual or rare "ornamentation" can make a person more
attractive and approachable to others. How can differentiation
be the formula to charm those around you?

"You were born an original.
Don't die a copy."

— **John Mason,**
Author

A 2014 STUDY LED BY Barnaby Dixson of the University of New South Wales found that in some cases, unusual or rare "ornamentation" such as beards in men makes the wearer more attractive to others. Steve Jobs, with his iconic black turtleneck and jeans, understood this principle. He liked the idea of having a uniform for himself, both because of the day-to-day convenience and its ability to convey a signature style that he came to be recognized for.

Comedian and talk show host Ellen DeGeneres is known for her well-tailored suits paired with sneakers. And serial entrepreneur Gary Vaynerchuk makes himself memorable with New York Jets attire—which also happens to be a reference to his lifelong goal of buying the Jets.

I have to wear a suit to work everyday, so I struggled to come up with my own signature style. But then I had an epiphany: pocket squares. They're small enough not to be obtrusive but still distinctive. I know they help me stand out, too—when the mailroom clerk had a package for me and asked around about who I was and where I sat, I overheard my colleague tell him, "He's the guy with the pocket square!"

THE TAKEAWAY: Differentiate yourself from others by standing out. Create a signature style, such as wearing a bow tie, that matches the character you are building.

EXERCISE
STAND OUT

Use differentiation as a formula to charm coworkers, friends and acquaintances. Make a list of potential signature styles.
Be creative!

● **WEAR COLORFUL SOCKS**
● **DRINK COFFEE OUT OF A STRANGE SHAPED MUG**
● **BRING YOUR DOG TO WORK**

What signature style can you apply to your life?

●
●
●
●
●
●
●

DAY #29

BECOME YOUR OWN PUBLICIST

Even the most powerful CEOs use "random" acts of kindness to raise awareness. How can you give people a reason to rave about you?

"We rise by lifting others."

— Robert Ingersoll,
Lawyer and Civil War veteran

DOUGLAS CONANT, FORMER CEO of Campbell Soup Company, always looked for opportunities to celebrate. He would scan his email and internal website to look for people who were contributing to his company so he could offer his appreciation. He even composed handwritten notes congratulating his employees on promotions. When Conant was in a car accident, hundreds of people returned the favor and inundated him with thank you notes.

Handwritten notes might not be Lady Gaga's M.O., but like Conant, Gaga is savvy about connecting to the people who make her career possible. She's a social media savant, constantly interacting with her fans online and advocating for their concerns. In return, her fans are remarkably loyal—something businesses and professionals should pay attention to.

For these kinds of efforts to work, though, they must be genuine. As Harvard Business School professor Bill George points out, being a good leader is less about trying to transform yourself into a different person as much as it is about honing the strengths you already have. In my experience, even small friendly gestures go a long way. When a co-worker announced she was leaving her job in sales to pursue an opportunity to become a news reporter, my department organized a farewell party. This was a very rare and exciting career move for my colleague, given that she didn't have much experience in the field, so I wanted to make her feel special—and give her and my colleagues a good laugh. Accordingly at the party I presented her with an inflatable purple microphone for practicing in the shower. My co-workers still laugh about it when they tell the story.

> **THE TAKEAWAY:** Celebrate your colleagues when they get a promotion, it's their birthday or they become engaged. One act of kindness can create an opportunity for people to talk about you in a positive way.

EXERCISE

BE KIND!

Kindness will help you build lasting impact on those around you. Think of a few colleagues; how can you show them good will (for example, helping with a task or sending a handwritten note on their birthday)?

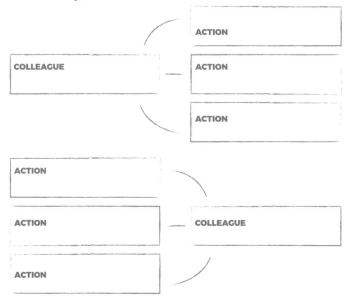

COLLEAGUE

ACTION

ACTION

ACTION

ACTION

ACTION

ACTION

COLLEAGUE

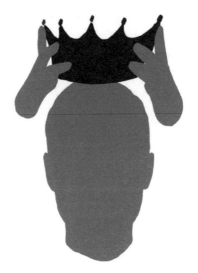

DAY #30

TREAT EVERYONE AS ROYALTY

It's true: Showing respect to others drives influence. How can you start expressing respect to everyone you see? Be humble. It's the most powerful weapon of influence.

> "A person is a person,
> no matter how small."

> **— Dr. Seuss,**
> Writer and cartoonist

ZARA FOUNDER AMANCIO ORTEGA is one of the wealthiest people in the world. But you wouldn't know it by looking at him. Ortega emerges from his apartment building in Spain most days wearing a simple blue blazer, white shirt and gray pants. He heads to the same coffee shop each morning and eats lunch alongside his employees in the Zara cafeteria.

Like Campbell Soup Company CEO Douglas Conant, Ortega has kept his profile low and his ear to the ground to stay connected with the people who make what he does possible. In many ways, he's the dictionary definition of humility, what psychologists describe as an awareness of your own limits.

If you demonstrate humility and respect to others, it can help you accomplish two goals, according to Harvard professor John Kotter: one, it enables you to soften whoever is in front of you, and two, it helps you win the broader audience around you.

I would add a third: Kindness is a revolving door. Every morning I greet my company's front desk officers by name and wish them a great day. Occasionally I bring them coffee. They know me and I know them, and we have established a relationship of mutual respect.

Those morning greetings saved my hide one afternoon when I went to lunch and left my badge ID at my desk. I returned from lunch running late for a very important presentation with no way to get through security without joining a long line. Luckily the front desk officers let me skip the security registration line because they knew me personally. I made it to the meeting on time—thanks to a simple "Good morning, Joe."

THE TAKEAWAY: Being humble is the most powerful weapon of influence. Treat everyone, from the janitor to the CEO, with the utmost respect. Be especially kind to office assistants—they will hook you up when you need help.

BE HUMBLE

If you give respect you'll immediately get it back. Use the rules you've learned in this book to start writing your own path. Make sure to listen to other people's stories, too!

LIVE LIKE FICTION!

That's it! Aim to use one of these tips each day, whether it's defining your daily goals or thinking about how to deal with unexpected situations.

Famed artists, inventors, executives, politicians, entrepreneurs—they didn't become the authors of their own stories totally by chance. They are experts at selling their ideas and explaining how they can impact the world. Knowingly or not, they Live Like Fiction. The ENGAGE formula will help you do that, too.

E: Explore your meaning
N: Narrow your goals
G: Generate a plan
A: Anticipate roadblocks
G: Gain endurance
E: Elevate yourself

Remember, this book welcomes more than one read, and you can always come back to it at each new chapter of your life. And please stay in touch with your "before and after" success stories.

Thank you

To my wife, Rachel, for inspiring me during the
journey of crafting this book.

To my parents, Francesco Sr. and Paula,
for encouraging me along the way.

To my publisher, Jason Ashlock, and the team at
Frontier Press who turned my fiction into reality.

To my book designer, Joona Leppänen,
for sharing his colors and creativity

To my copy editor, Kelsey Michael,
for reviewing my neverending drafts.

•••

To my friends who supported me in this project including Jessica Geist, Seth Harris, Marty Swant, Randy Smith, Jake Kreinberg, Adam Fachler, Neil Strauss, Nick Michael, Jim Kennedy, Kate Lee, Jack Becht, Eric Fisher, Matt Brimer, Miklos Sarvary, Andrew Heyward, Adam Klein, Bill Grueskin and all the folks at Malta do Costume.

READINGS THAT INSPIRED ME

Ellen Langer, Maja Djikic, Michael Pirson, Arin Madenci, Rebecca Donohue (2010). Believing Is Seeing: Using Mindlessness (Mindfully) to Improve Visual Acuity. Journal of Psychological Science

Martin Seligman (2004). Authentic Happiness: Using the New Positive Psychology to Realize your Potential for Lasting Fulfillment. Atria Books

Crystal Hoyt, Jeni Burnette, and Audrey Innella (2012). I Can Do That: The Impact of Implicit Theories on Leadership Role Model Effectiveness. Personality and Social Psychology Bulletin

Trevor Blake (2012). Three Simple Steps: A Map to Success in Business and Life. BenBella Books

Ernest L. Abel, Michael L. Kruger (2010). Smile Intensity in Photographs Predicts Longevity. Journal of Psychological Science.

Jennifer Aaker, Andy Smith (2010). The Dragonfly Effect: Quick, Effective, and Powerful Ways To Use Social. Jossey-Bass

Gail Mattthews (2015). Research Study on Strategies for Achieving Goals. Conference of the Psychology Research Unit of Athens Institute for Education and Research.

Staples Advantage (2016). Workplace Index Survey.

Piotr Winkielman, Liam Kavanagh, Christopher Suhler, Patricia Churchland (2011). When it's an Error to Mirror: The Surprising Reputational Costs of Mimicry. Journal of Psychological Science.

Alexander Todorov, Christopher Y. Olivola, Ron Dotsch, Peter Mende-Siedlecki (2015). Social Attributions from Faces: Determinants, Consequences, Accuracy, and Functional Significance. Annual Review of Phycology.

Lauren Rivera (2012). Hiring as Cultural Matching the Case of Elite Professional Service Firms. American Sociological Review.

Jonah Berger (2016). Contagious: Why Things Catch On. Simon & Schuster.

Andrew Przybylskia, Kou Murayamab , Cody DeHaanc , Valerie Gladwelld (2013). Motivational, Emotional, and Behavioral Correlates of Fear of Missing out. Computers in Human Behavior.

Tim Pychyl, JM Lee, Rachelle Thibodeau, Allan Blunt (2000). Five Days of Emotion: An Experience Sampling Study of Undergraduate Student Procrastination. Journal of Social Behavior and Personality

Timothy Judge, Beth Livingston. (2011). Do Nice Guys—and Gals—Really Finish Last? The Joint Effects of Sex and Agreeableness on Income. Journal of Personality and Social Psychology

Adam Grant, Francesca Gino (2010). A Little Thanks Goes a Long Way: Explaining Why Gratitude Expressions Motivate Prosocial Behavior. Journal of Personality and Social Psychology.

Diana Tamir, Jason P. Mitchell (2012). Disclosing Information About the Self is Intrinsically Rewarding. Proceedings of the National Academy of Science.

Robert Cialdini (2006). Influence: The Psychology of Persuasion. Harper Business.

James Fowler, Nicholar Cristakis (2010). Cooperative Behavior Cascades in Human Social Networks. Proceedings of the National Academy of Sciences.

Kevin J. Eschleman, Jamie Madsen, Gene Alarcon, Alex Barelka (2014). Benefiting from Creative Activity: The Positive Relationships Between Creative Activity, Recovery Experiences, and Performance-Related Outcomes. Journal of Occupational and Organizational Psychology

Vijay Eswaran (2015). In the Sphere of Silence. RYTHM House.

Mary Czerwinski, Eric Horvitz, Susan Wilhite (2008). A Diary Study of Task Switching and Interruptions. Microsoft Research.

Sheena Iyengar (2010). The Art of Choosing. Twelve.

Saras D. Sarasvathy (2001). What Makes Entrepreneurs Entrepreneurial? University of Virginia - Darden School of Business.

David Lynch Foundation (2010). The Quiet Program: Restoring a Positive Culture of Academics and Well-being in High-need School Communities. The San Francisco Unified School District.

Kristin Layous , S. Katherine Nelson, Eva Oberle, Kimberly A. Schonert-Reichl, Sonja Lyubomirsky (2012). Kindness Counts: Prompting Prosocial Behavior in Preadolescents Boosts Peer Acceptance and Well-Being. PLOS ONE.

John J Skowronski, Donal E Carlston, Lynda Mae, Matthew T. Crawford (1998). Spontaneous Trait Transference: Communicators Take on the Qualities they Describe in Others. Journal of Personality and Social Psychology,

Barnaby Dixson, Paul Vasey (2012). Beards Augment Perceptions of Men's age, Social Status, and Aggressiveness, but not Attractiveness. Behavioral Ecology

Bill George (2003). Authentic Leadership: Rediscovering the Secrets to Creating Lasting Value. Jossey-Bass.

Pelin Kesebir (2014). A Quiet Ego Quiets Death Anxiety: Humility as an Existential Anxiety Buffer. Journal of Personality and Social Psychology